T0308192

Teams Work Together

CONTENTS

NATIONAL GEOGRAPHIC
School Publishing
Hampton-Brown

ur
er
ir

Words with er, ir, ur

Look at each picture. Read the words.

Example:

girl

curl

fern

shirt

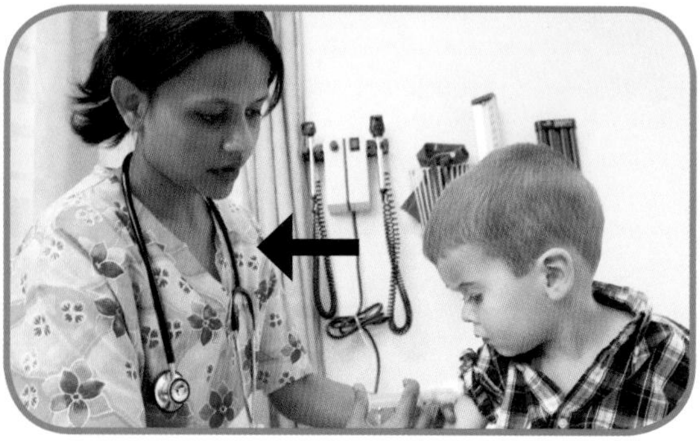

nurse

perch

High Frequency Words

- always
- boy
- brother
- gave
- myself
- pull
- sister
- took
- upon
- us

Key Words

Read the sentences. Match each sentence to one of the pictures.

Help

1. Once **upon** a time, a **boy** had a job to do.
2. "I **always** do it **myself**," he said.
3. He **took** hold of the rope, **gave** a tug, and began to **pull**.
4. "You need **us**!" said his **brother** and **sister**.

What will the boy think the next time he has a big load to pull?

Phonics Games
NGReach.com

Gert Does It Herself

by Will Jimmerson
illustrated by Julia Woolf

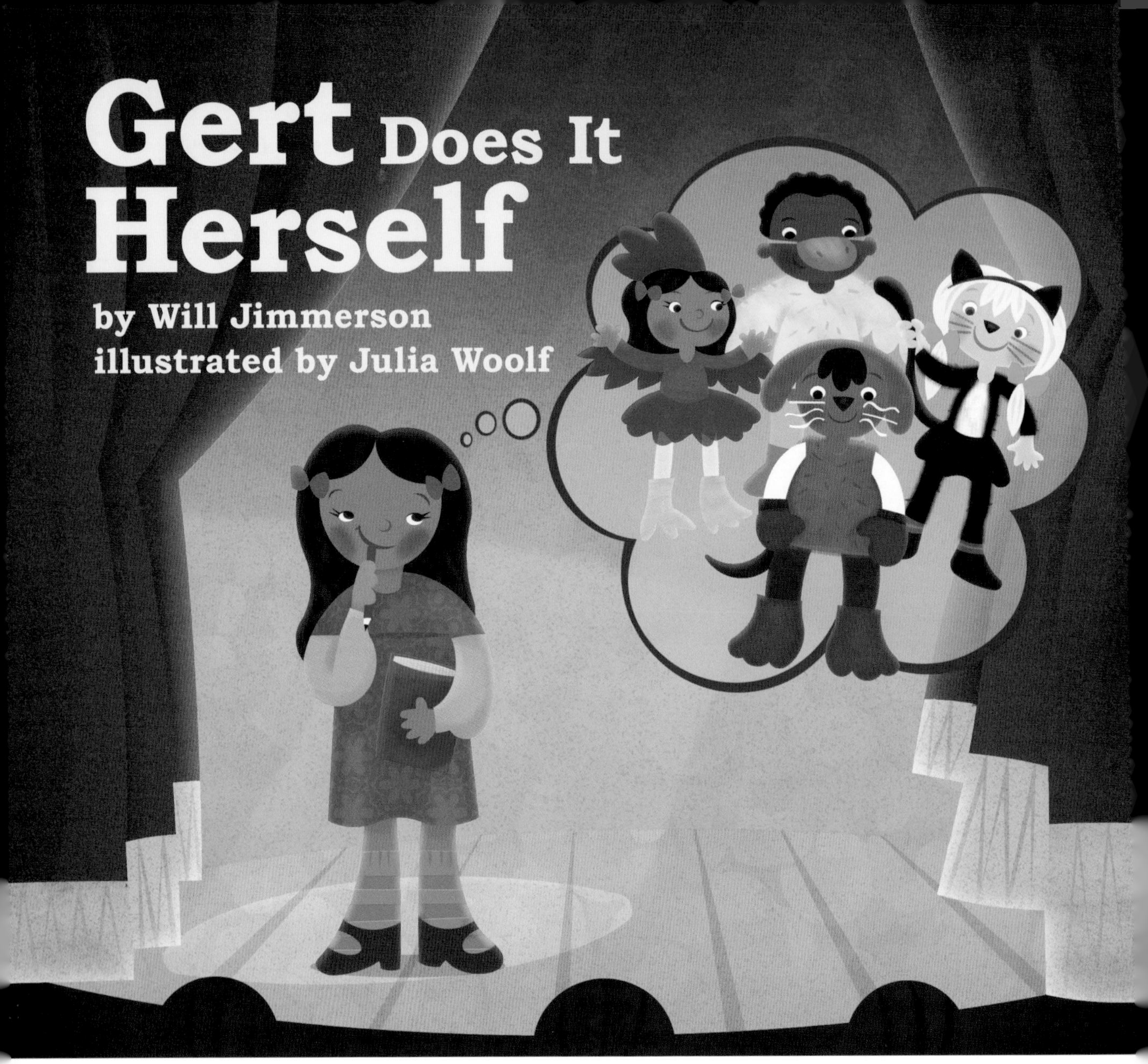

Gert had written a play called *The Little Red Hen*. She wanted to stage it at school. She'd be the Little Red Hen. She gave her friends the other roles.

"We have lots to do. First, who will make costumes?" Gert asked.

"Not me," said Curtis. "I have to work on my barking." He was the Dog.

“Not me,” said Shirl. “I have to work on my purring.” She was the Cat.

“I have to work on my quacking,” said Herb. He was the Duck.

“Then I’ll do it myself,” said Gert. “Second, who can paint scenery?”

“Not me!” said Curtis. And Shirl. And Herb.

“Then I’ll do it myself,” muttered Gert.

"Third," said Gert, "who can sell tickets?"

"You're so good at selling things," said Herb. The rest nodded.

Once more, Gert had to do it herself.

At home, Gert perched upon her bed. The girl was hurt. Her friends always expected her to do all the work.

"Why must I always say I'll do it myself?" she blurted. "I *am* the Little Red Hen—in real life!"

She sighed and began planning costumes. Should Duck be in a yellow shirt and have bird wings? Should Cat have a fur skirt?

Her sister and brother found her hard at work.

"We're going to the zoo. Come with us!" her sister urged.

Her brother tried to pull Gert off the bed. "You need to have fun!" the boy cried.

But Gert was firm. "I can't. I need to work!"

She was planning scenery when her friends burst in.

Curtis picked up Gert's costume sketches. "These are cool!" he said. "I've got my team all set to make them."

Shirl took the scenery plans. “My turn to help,” she said. “I’ve got a team, too!”

Herb perched beside Gert. “I’ve got kids who can help us sell tickets,” he said. “We’ll make posters, too, and tack them up in stores.”

"Gert, we acted like real jerks," said Shirl. The rest nodded.

"I'm not the Little Red Hen now!" Gert cried. "I'm part of a team!"

Words with <u>er</u>, <u>ir</u>, <u>ur</u>

Read these words.

girl	jerks	turns	perches
boy	cat	bird	purrs

Find words with **er**, **ir**, and **ur**. Use letters to build them.

g i r l

Talk Together

The cat purrs.

These kids are putting on a show. Choose words from the box above. Tell your partner what each kid does.

ur
er
ir

Longer Words with er, ir, ur

Look at each picture. Read the word.

Example:

th**ir**teen

b**ur**g**er**

f**ur**ry

p**er**fume

hamst**er**

c**ir**cus

High Frequency Words
always
boy
brother
gave
myself
pull
sister
took
upon
us

Key Words

Read the sentences. Match each sentence to one of the pictures.

Team of Three

1. Once **upon** a time, a **boy** grew a radish.
2. "I can't **pull** it out **myself**," he said.
3. His **brother** and **sister** **took** over, but they **gave** up and cried, "Help **us**!"
4. It **always** helps to have a big team!

Why does it always help to have a big team?

Phonics Games

NGReach.com

The Enormous Turnip

retold by Joanna Korba
illustrated by Virginia Allyn

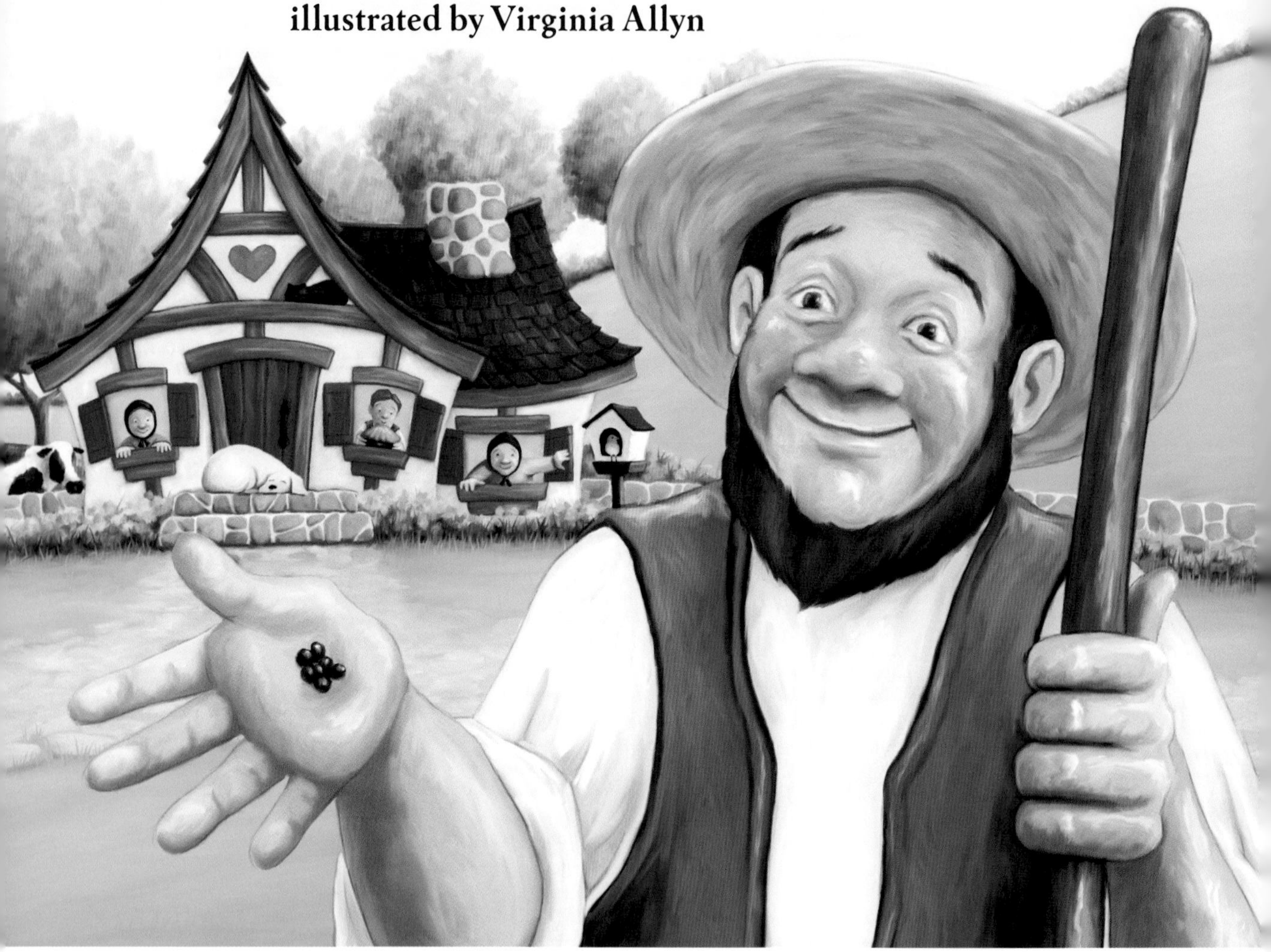

Once upon a time, a farmer named Murphy found some turnip seeds. "These will be a nice surprise for my family," he murmured. "I'll plant and tend them myself."

He always gave the thirsty seeds plenty of water. But after a while, only one seedling had burst through the dirt. Still, Farmer Murphy was not the sort of person to be sad.

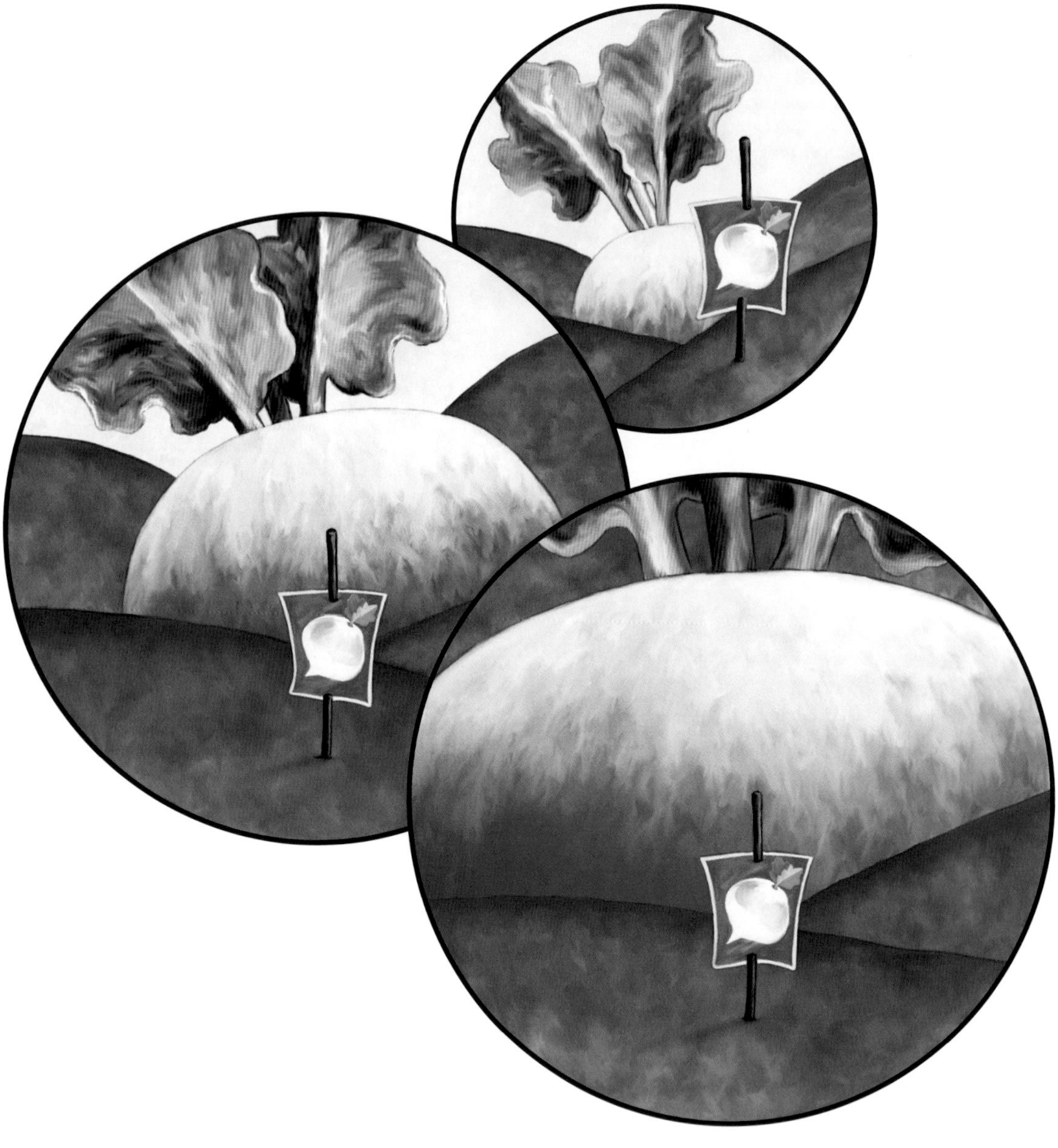

He was happy to tend his little turnip. Soon it got large. Then it got huge. By summer's end, it was enormous. He had to pull the turnip out.

So Farmer Murphy took hold . . .

He grabbed . . . and tugged . . . and snorted.
The turnip did not budge.

"Help me, Wife!" he yelled.

She hurried over and grabbed his waist.

Together, they yanked . . . and tugged . . . and grunted. The turnip did not budge.

"Help us, Bernard!" they yelled to their son.

The boy hurried over and grabbed his mom's waist.

Together, they gripped . . . and dragged . . . and groaned. The turnip did not budge.

"Help us, Gertrude!" they yelled.

Bernard's sister hurried over and grabbed her brother's waist.

Together, they jerked . . . and strained . . . and sighed. The turnip did not budge.

"Help us, Sherman!" they yelled.

Their dog raced over and grabbed Gertrude's skirt.

Together, they clutched . . . and struggled . . . and squealed. The turnip did not budge.

"Help us, Germaine!" they yelled.

Their cat rushed over and grabbed Sherman's tail.

Together, they reached . . . and stretched . . . and screamed. The turnip did not budge.

"Help us, Kermit!" they yelled.

Their bluebird fluttered over and grabbed Germaine's tail.

Together, they wrenched . . . and twisted . . . and screeched.

POP! The enormous turnip burst free!

The team dragged the dirty turnip inside. Together, they cleaned it, cut it up, and baked it.

They sat in a circle around the table. It felt like they were at a birthday party.

"We make a perfect team!" cried Farmer Murphy. "Let's eat!"

Longer Words with er, ir, ur

Read these words.

dirty	person	beaver	turnip
gerbil	chewing	scurrying	thirsty

Find words with **er**, **ir**, and **ur**.
Use letters to build them.

d i r t y

Talk Together

Choose words from the box above to tell your partner what you see in this garden.

The beaver is chewing.

A Surprise Birthday Party

Some friends gave their friend a surprise birthday party. Look at the picture. Take turns reading the clues and pointing to the answers.

1. Find a girl with a red purse.
2. Find the person who is surprised.
3. Find the boy with a purple shirt.
4. Find the bird that sits upon a perch looking at us.
5. Find the brother and sister who are dressed alike.

Acknowledgments
Grateful acknowledgment is given to the authors, artists, photographers, museums, publishers, and agents for permission to reprint copyrighted material. Every effort has been made to secure the appropriate permission. If any omissions have been made or if corrections are required, please contact the Publisher.

Photographic Credits
CVR Artiga Photo/Corbis. **2** (bl) Frank Siteman/Science Faction/Corbis. (br) ene/Shutterstock. (cl) Norma Cornes/Shutterstock. (cr) Roman Sigaev/Shutterstock. (tl) David Buffington/Getty Images. (tr) Heather Weston/Getty Images. **3** Liz Garza Williams/Hampton-Brown/National Geographic School Publishing. **15** Liz Garza Williams/Hampton-Brown/National Geographic School Publishing. **16** (bl) Feng Yu/iStockphoto. (br) Visions of America, LLC/Alamy Images. (cl) Kirill Vorobyev/Shutterstock. (cr) Stockbyte/Getty Images. (tr) Filipe B. Varela/Shutterstock. **17** Liz Garza Williams/Hampton-Brown/National Geographic School Publishing. **29** Liz Garza Williams/Hampton-Brown/National Geographic School Publishing.

Illustrator Credits
3, 15, 17, 29 Peter Grosshauer; **4-14** Julia Woolf; **18-28** Virginia Allyn; **30-31** Mattia Cerato

National Geographic School Publishing
Hampton-Brown
www.NGSP.com

Printed in the USA.
Quad Graphics, Leominster, MA

ISBN:978-0-7362-8078-5

17 18 19
10 9 8